35

plurals
(s, es)

le

# The Lucky Penny

by Dina McClellan
Illustrated by Cary Pillo

SCHOLASTIC INC.
New York  Toronto  London  Auckland  Sydney

It was a great day for the park.
Jim had it all planned out.

"First we swim," he said.
"Then we eat. I brought some
good things to nibble on. After
that we can play paddle ball."

Ricky wanted to come, too, but Mom said "No." She wanted him to stay home and rest. Ricky had a cold and a sniffle.

There are three of us—Ricky, Jim, and me. Ricky is the little one. He has a dimple when he smiles.

Jim is the biggest. He thinks he knows it all.

I'm in the middle. My name is Jill.

Jim got our pool passes and our towels.
"We need to take two buses," he said.
"Do you have any money?"

I grabbed my backpack and made it jingle.
I had a lot of dimes. I had a lot of nickels.
I had—no pennies.

No pennies!

"Oh no!" I groaned. "My lucky penny! It's
lost!"

I checked again. And again.

"Wait, Jim!" I called. "We can't go yet. My lucky penny is lost!"

"Are you sure?" said Jim. "It must be there."

"It is not," I said. "I looked twice. This is where I always keep it. It's lost."

Jim put his bag down. "Then let's find it," he said.

"*I'll* find it," said Ricky. "I'm the best at finding things."

If you know me, you know about my bright, shiny, lucky penny. It has always brought me good luck.

I take it with me every day.

My lucky penny never lets me down.

Here's one example.

I had my penny at the school play. Even though we got there late, we got good seats. Ricky and I sat right in front.

Here's another example.

I had my penny at the math test.

Even though the test was hard, it seemed simple.

I got ten out of ten right.

And here's another example.

I had my penny at the Dog Show.

Even though Sparkle would not *sit*, we were the winners. We got first place.

But where was my penny now?

"I bet I know where it is," said Jim.
He rushed to the front room. Ricky was
right behind him. "Lots of things get lost
down here." Jim said. He picked up a
pillow from the couch.

Ricky zoomed across the room. He darted in front of Jim. Then Ricky threw pillows all over the place. "Here, penny, penny! Where are you, penny?" he yelled.

Jim and I started to giggle. Ricky looked at us with a big grin. "Hey!" he said.

"Look what I've got!"

"That's the way to go, Ricky!" I shouted.
I ran over to get my lucky penny.
It wasn't my penny, though. It was a
part of a jigsaw puzzle.

"Wow!" said Jim. "That's been lost for
weeks."

"Good old Ricky," said Ricky.

"It's from the puzzle Uncle Bill
brought me," said Jim. "I didn't know
where it could be. Thanks, Ricky.
Now that puzzle won't be such a mess."

"Yes," said Ricky. "Lucky lucky."

It *was* lucky. But where was my
penny?

"I bet I know where it is," said Jim.
He walked over to the table. There was a
pile of things on top. I always put my
odds and ends there. Jim started to look
through the jumble.

He picked up a rattle and gave it a
shake.

# Ocean
# Explorers

# Contents

# Features

The Vikings were sailors from long ago. They lived in northern Europe. Turn to page 7 to learn what the word *Viking* really means.

When did people first discover and settle islands in the Pacific Ocean? Turn to page 8 to learn about these amazing adventurers.

How can a captain know exactly where a ship is at sea? Find out how technology helps ocean explorers on page 18.

An adventurous teenager recently became the youngest person to sail alone around the world. Read **A Spirit of Adventure** on page 20 to find out who he is.

**Learn how to build your own model ship.**

Visit **www.rigbyinfoquest.com**
for more about SHIPS AND SAILING.

# The World Unknown

The oceans are waters of adventure and discovery. For many years, explorers have sailed across wild seas in search of new lands.

They set sail in many kinds of ships. They didn't always know where their journey would take them. They returned with new knowledge that helped build a better picture of the world. Slowly, the mapping of Earth's real land and sea began to take shape.

ALASKA

CANADA

NORTH AMERIC

PACIFIC OCEAN

Strait Mage

Viking longship

Polynesian canoe

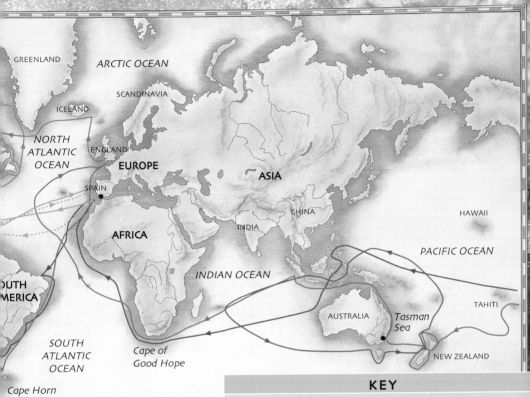

| | KEY | |
|---|---|---|
| | **Explorer** | **Year** |
| —— | Leif Erikson | 1000–1001 |
| | Christopher Columbus | |
| —— | First voyage | 1492–1493 |
| - - - | Fourth voyage | 1502–1504 |
| —— | Voyage begun by Ferdinand Magellan | 1519–1522 |
| —— | Henry Hudson | 1610 |
| —— | Abel Tasman | 1642–1644 |
| —— | James Cook's first voyage | 1768–1771 |

Mapmakers, or **cartographers,** have made a better picture of the world with each new voyage and discovery.

Chinese junk

Clipper

# The Viking Explorers

Viking sailors from Sweden, Denmark, and Norway were among the earliest ocean explorers. The Vikings were good sailors and shipbuilders. They made strong, fast ships from wood. They loaded their ships with **cargo** such as furs to trade and set off, hoping to discover more land.

Many people were afraid of these Viking warriors who sailed stormy seas and were ready to fight.

A famous Viking explorer named Leif Erikson was the first person from Europe to land in North America. He landed over 1,000 years ago.

GREENLAND

ICELAND

FAEROE
ISLANDS

VINLAND

NORWAY

SWEDEN

DENMARK

Baltic
Sea

Dnieper River

Volga River

Kiev

NORMANDY

Caspian
Sea

Luna

Black Sea

SPAIN

Miklagård
(Constantinople)

Seville

To Baghdad

Mediterranean
Sea

WORD BUILDER

The Vikings attacked many
of the lands they discovered.
The word *Viking* comes
from a Norse word
meaning "piracy."

# The Island Adventurers

While the Vikings explored northern seas, people from Polynesia were exploring the huge Pacific Ocean. With their families, they paddled across the sea in long, strong canoes full of **produce** such as bananas and coconuts. These sailors had nothing to guide them but the patterns of the stars and the rhythms of the ocean currents. They discovered and settled many new lands.

TIME LINK

Year 400

People from Polynesia settle Easter Island in the Pacific.

Year 600

Polynesians settle the Hawaiian islands.

Year 750

Polynesians arrive in New Zealand.

SOUTHEAST ASIA

PHILIPPINES

MALAYSIA

INDONESIA

New Guinea

AUSTRALIA

Hawaii

POLYNESIA

Samoa

Cook Islands

Marquesas Islands

Fiji

Tahiti

Tonga

Society Islands

Easter Island

PACIFIC OCEAN

NEW ZEALAND

Chatham Islands

WORD BUILDER

This southern part of the world is now called *Polynesia*. The name Polynesia means "many islands."

1642

Ocean explorer Abel Tasman, from Europe, arrives in New Zealand.

1779

Captain James Cook reaches Hawaii.

9

# Land Ahoy!

Land was a welcome sight for men and women who had been at sea for months at a time. One of the longest sea voyages was in 1492 when the explorer Christopher Columbus sailed west from Spain with a **fleet** of ships. Columbus reached a great and rich land area— the Americas. He thought he had found Asia, but he landed in what was soon called the New World.

The *Santa Maria*, shown here, was Columbus' special **flagship.**

1  Crow's-nest

2  Captain's cabin

3  Upper deck

4  Food stores

New
World

Spain

ATLANTIC
OCEAN

Columbus crossed
the stormy Atlantic
Ocean four times.

# Galleons of Gold

The Spanish set sail for the rich New World early in the 1500s. They crossed the ocean in great ships called **galleons.** They were greedy for the treasures of the New World, so they filled their ships with gold and jewels from the areas of Mexico and Peru.

Pirates often attacked the galleons to take their treasure. The seas became dangerous with the criss-crossing of ships and swords. But from this time on, people began to sail to all parts of the world.

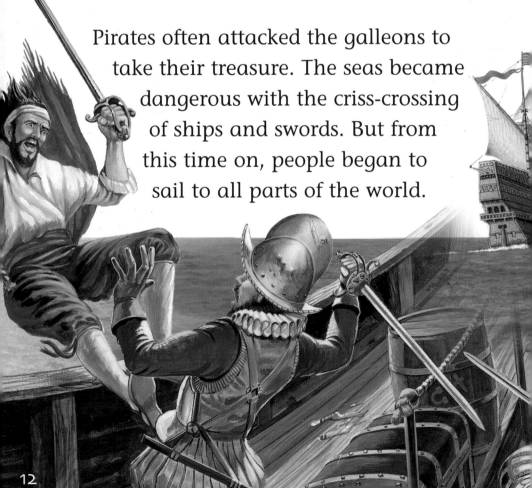

1519

A famous explorer from Portugal named Ferdinand Magellan was the first person to lead a voyage around the world. His journey proved once and for all that Earth is round.

# Tall Tales

Sailors saw many surprising sights during their travels. They also faced many dangers. Sometimes danger came as a mighty storm, jagged rocks, or high seas. Sometimes it was the mystery and fear of the unknown. Sailors often told tales of terrible sea monsters, singing mermaids, and wicked pirates. As they traveled from port to port, the stories grew beyond the truth to become larger than life.

Pirates began attacking and robbing ships in very early times. Some pirates of the past, such as Blackbeard, became so famous that they live on today as **legends.** Stories about pirates are still popular. They sometimes give the wrong idea that pirates lived only in the past. In fact, pirates still rob ships in parts of the world today. The word pirate means "sea robber."

# Icebreakers

The icy waters of the North Atlantic Ocean were the most dangerous parts of the world for early ocean explorers. Here, sailors saw icebergs as big as skyscrapers. They had to **navigate** through freezing waters of jagged ice. Sometimes ships were trapped in the ice for months. The crew would run out of fresh food and become ill with a disease called **scurvy.**

Special ships called icebreakers are used today to make passages through thick ice for other ships.

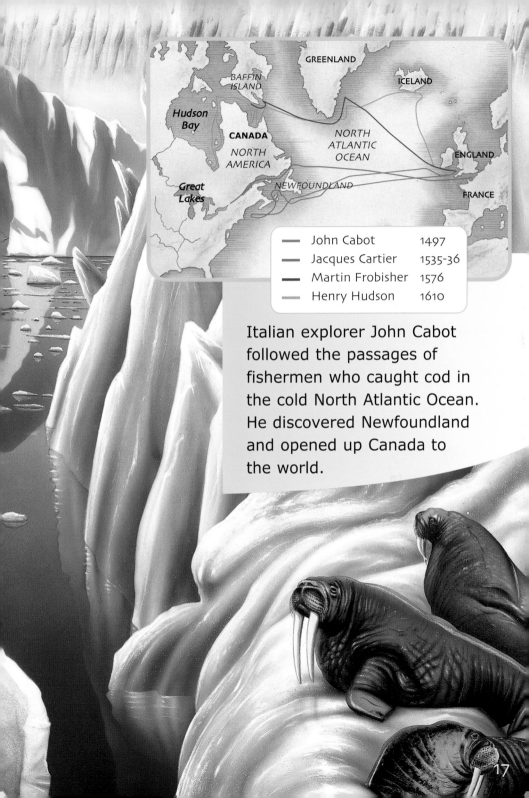

GREENLAND

BAFFIN
ISLAND

ICELAND

Hudson
Bay

CANADA

NORTH
ATLANTIC
OCEAN

ENGLAND

NORTH
AMERICA

Great
Lakes

NEWFOUNDLAND

FRANCE

— John Cabot 1497
— Jacques Cartier 1535-36
— Martin Frobisher 1576
— Henry Hudson 1610

Italian explorer John Cabot followed the passages of fishermen who caught cod in the cold North Atlantic Ocean. He discovered Newfoundland and opened up Canada to the world.

# Sailing the High Seas

Today ships of all shapes and sizes cross the world's oceans. Container ships carry cargo around the world. Huge, fancy ships carry people to many countries. There are fishing boats, sailing boats, racing boats, and rescue boats. The captains of these vessels do not have to navigate by the stars. High-tech tools tell them where they are and help to keep them going in the right direction.

**TECHTALK**

It once took great time and effort for early explorers to figure out where they were at sea. Today, a satellite computer system called The Global Positioning System (G.P.S.) displays a ship's position when the captain presses a button.

18

Container ship

Rescue boat

TEER COASTGUARD

CUE 1

Fishing boat

Receiver

Satellite

G.P.S. display monitor

# A Spirit of Adventure

People no longer find new lands or need new sea paths, but the oceans are still grand places of adventure and discovery.

For today's young explorers like Jesse Martin, the seas are very inviting. On December 7, 1998, Jesse set off from Melbourne, Australia to sail alone around the world. His journey lasted 328 days. Seabirds and seals were the only company for this 17-year-old sailor filled with a spirit of adventure.

## Map of Jesse's Journey

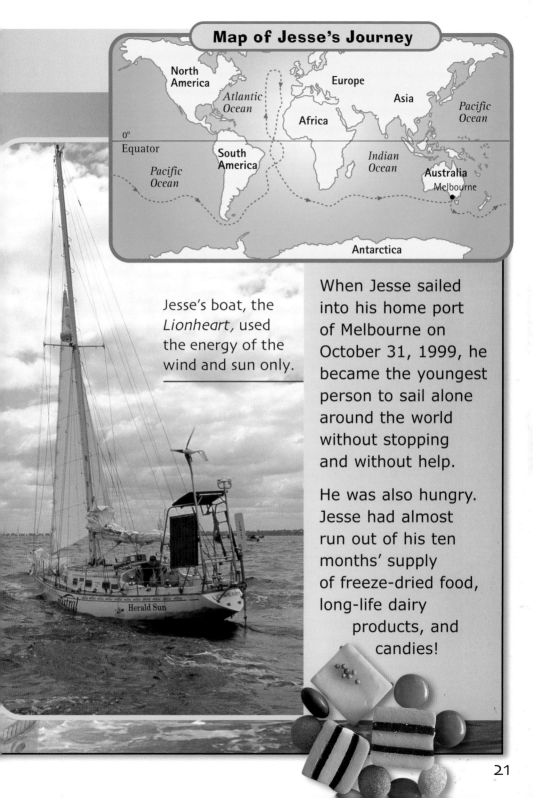

North America

Europe

Asia

*Atlantic Ocean*

Africa

*Pacific Ocean*

0°
Equator

South America

*Indian Ocean*

*Pacific Ocean*

Australia
Melbourne

Antarctica

Jesse's boat, the *Lionheart,* used the energy of the wind and sun only.

When Jesse sailed into his home port of Melbourne on October 31, 1999, he became the youngest person to sail alone around the world without stopping and without help.

He was also hungry. Jesse had almost run out of his ten months' supply of freeze-dried food, long-life dairy products, and candies!

# Glossary

**cargo** – the load that a ship carries. Ships carry cargo such as food and cars.

**cartographer** – a person who makes maps. Cartographers use lines, colors, shapes, and symbols to design maps.

**flagship** – a ship that carries the leader of a fleet of ships. A flagship flies a special flag to show that person is on board.

**fleet** – a group of ships traveling together and all under the control of one leader

**galleon** – a heavy, wooden sailing ship with square sails used long ago

**legend** – an old story based on something real but changed so all of it is no longer true

**navigate** – to steer a ship or boat and find a way across water

**produce** – fresh fruit and vegetables

**scurvy** – a disease that early sailors often suffered on long sea voyages. Scurvy is caused by a lack of Vitamin C, which is in fresh fruit and vegetables.

# Index

# Discussion Starters

**1** If someone is going to sail the world alone, what planning would need to be done ahead of time? What should be taken along? Why?

**2** If you had been at sea for months and months and at long last stepped onto dry land, what is the first thing you would do? What would you have missed most about the land?

**3** Explorers have now discovered and mapped most of Earth. Where might there still be hidden and unknown lands to explore? What do you think they might be like?